D1626979

The Death of Long Steam Lady

by
Nellie Wong

PS
3573
.O5813
D42
1986

Thanks to the editors of the following publications in which many of these poems first appeared:

American Born and Foreign (Sunbury 7/8), Bridge, Asian American Perspectives, Dear Gentlepersons: A Collection of Bay Area Poets, Echoes from Gold Mountain, The Freedom Socialist Newspaper, Hanging Loose, The Journal of Ethnic Studies, Real Fiction, Prisma, Room, The Sow's Ear, This Bridge Called My Back: Writings by Radical Women of Color, 13th Moon, Ikon 4, Between Our Selves: Women of Color Newspaper, The Iowa Review, Alcatraz/2, Breaking Silence: An Anthology of Contemporary Asian American Poets, Daughter to Mother.

Thanks to Allie Light and Irving Saraf, producers of the documentary film, "Mitsuye and Nellie, Asian American Poets," in which excerpts of "It's In The Blood" were first broadcast.

Book design: Liz Jan
Photo: Lou Dematteis

First edition – September, 1986.
ISBN 0-931122-42-2.

This project is partially supported by a grant from the California Arts Council, a State Agency.

West End Press, P.O. Box 291477, Los Angeles, CA 90029.

TABLE OF CONTENTS

SONG FROM DARK

WHEN I WAS GROWING UP

IT'S IN THE BLOOD

RED JOURNEYS

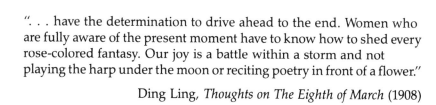

". . . have the determination to drive ahead to the end. Women who are fully aware of the present moment have to know how to shed every rose-colored fantasy. Our joy is a battle within a storm and not playing the harp under the moon or reciting poetry in front of a flower."

Ding Ling, *Thoughts on The Eighth of March* (1908)

Dedicated to the memory of Leslie Jow, blood-sister, friend, community activist, and intransigent fighter, who taught me that change is possible if we stand up and fight back with courage, commitment and love.

Song from Dark

TERRITORIAL VISIONS

Sometimes the longing is living, sometimes the indolence of sleep.
Dragons prowl, whirl from the sea into my dreams
and I am safe, enclosed from the periphery of the inkblue sky.
A sailboat in the distance is merely a speck,
its movement mousequick as I slide further down.
Turning inward the petals of night,
the horizon blooms a thousand flowers.
Aloneness is being of the body.
Wakefulness, deceptive as mirrors, and my spheres clash.
Prehistoric animals roamed the previous civilizations.
Then, too, I was afraid lying beneath the earth's crust.
What matter is my body, my mind, what essence
in this universe at the electric typewriter,
the steady hum of the airconditioner?
Cars and trucks curve endlessly into skyscrapers
and the noon hour moves, a tiger stalking the stillness.
Lying and dreaming.   Tossing,
turning and stretching, my arms attempt to fly from my body.
Where can I race, can I run, to return
to where I am, to explore where I've never been?
Fingering the pages I slip into the past
and lift my feet with the bobolinks.

ODE TO TWO SISTERS IN THE SUN

Inspired by a Chinese folktale
where two sisters who lived in
the moon exchanged places with
their brother who lived in the sun.

When I eye the sun, I do not know.
Is it you two ladies sewing in your sun palace?
Is it you who prick my eyes with seventy needles,
fireworks bursting
the sky wide open?

Your silks, your embroideries overflow.
I pull your fabrics thread by thread
and still you speak no language
no dialect I understand.

You exchange places with your brother in the sun.
You obey the precepts
enact the virtues of modesty and shame.
The men on rooftops, in silent courtyards
expose your beauty, the power
that no one can pierce
and no one can deny.

Two sisters, will you speak out?
Will you enlighten the universe,
saturate our tongues with song?

Why did your brother go willingly
to live in the moon?
Why haven't I seen you
these long lost years?

I ride a moonboat across the sky
from beyond the sea
to the sun, your home.

Will I recognize you when we meet
and will our singing, our linking of hands
see me safely home?

4

AND FOR THEIR TOMORROW

Tomorrow when the cock crows,
I will arise
and wash the sleep from my eyes.
I will put on new cotton slippers
and wait in the common hall
for my husband to fetch me.

Riding in the palanquin
my face will be shielded
from my uncles and aunts
and the dirt road
I know so well
will swallow my footprints.

And when I have lain
with my husband
for the first time,
I do not know
if I will understand
the hissing of his snake.
I do not know
if I will understand
my moonflower's bursting.

And the next tomorrow
when the cock crows,
I will arise and fetch water
and brew father-in-law's tea.

I will arise
and fetch water
and wash mother-in-law's feet.

I will arise
and cook rice
for brother-in-law's breakfast.

I will arise
and sew new pants
for sister-in-law's approval.

And for their tomorrow
when the cock crows,
my parents, my sisters and brothers
will arise
and will eat
the grain and rice
threshed from my body,
the undeclared price
of my meager dowry.

RIDE

You ride the waves of the yellow sea,
your limbs melting like ice cream in July.

What's happened to the stir fried chicken
you cooked so well?

You hang on to the raft,
the sea sweeping you into the storm.

You look up and see a tree,
your lungs
hanging there
like barbecued ribs.

Oh! If you could only reach,
you would serve them to your sons,
unadulterated,
not even plum sauced.

YOU CALL

You call my name, Neh-leeeee, Neh-leeeee,
your voice subdued as mellow wine
and I jump from the kangaroo's pocket
to be your walking cane.

I, a glutinous riceball, stick to you
for if I sour, you will latch on
to the moon
in your night flight.

In your bath you turn from me
not because your breasts are tiny buttons
not because your dresses fit the fat lady
at the circus, but because
you wear your modesty
a necklace of jade.

What do I say
when your neighbors ask about you?
Why do they ask me
when they live next door?
Have they abandoned you like a little bitch
whose urine is dark as beets?

But there are angels
(or are angels Chinese?)
who cook your rice gruel as they too
wade in heated streams.

Ah, but do they not need you
as you need them
and have you not hooked up in space,
brushstrokes flooding the skies,
waiting for your own inkwells
to be filled?

SONG FROM DARK

Dark woman, I hear you
cough
snatches of air
unaromatic
unlike cigars.
Come here to this room,
this bed
covered with handquilted rags.
Although this room is small,
it is yours,
your eyes
I cannot ignore.
Here on the top floor
in this building
dialects drift from patches
of jade plant, through peanut-oiled halls.
Where do you belong,
if not here?
Your skeletal frame
attracts my rough hands,
seeking relief
in the shapes of clouds.
Never mind the others,
their superstitions
packed in cans
of dried salted fish.
I will burn incense,
bake mooncakes.
Now that you're here,
you focus on my Chinese evergreen,
illuminating the lesions on my skin.
Will you eat, will you eat
if I feed you rice gruel
through paper straws,
these outstretched hands?

DAUGHTERS, SONS

You are my daughters, my sons.
Tell me I am your mother.
Tell me as I sit in this forest,
shadows of light shine on my body,
my flesh weathered like wood fungus.

Tell me so the trees
will know me.

My hands are tied.
The trees do not speak
but I memorize them.
They are all I have.

Your father did nothing to harm me.
He planted me and I grew
you,
fingers of silence,
odorless and warm.

Now I want to see
your father's first wife,
her bones,
the one you still call
"Mother."
Now I want to know:
What characters
will you carve
on my headstone?

HARBINGER

In the March winds my mother comes to me.
She is the sunlight piercing my eyes,
she is the breeze caressing my cheeks.
In braided red yarn she flies,
no wings, no gold teeth.
Eyebrows penciled a fine line.
Her feet grip this brown earth.
She might be sixteen.

Eight years ago I sat with my mother,
sixty five, at her blue formica table
in her fifth floor apartment
and I asked what she thought
when she saw my father
for the very first time.

My mother looked down, blushed
like a young bride,
not knowing she emerged
a harbinger of wedding sons
to her children and grandchildren
who filled her arms:
How lucky, how lucky
to be born in America,
how she was born too soon,
how her luck clouded
beneath the stars,
how it had been decreed
through precepts, through rituals
she would work to bone.

How she insisted
I listen to her very words,
how I closed my ears thinking:
She is only my mother.

And now rainclouds overhead
move like a serpent
breathing fire
into my fingers, piercing my heart.

MAMA, COME BACK

Mama, come back.
Why did you leave
now that I am learning you?
The landlady next door
how she apologizes
for my rough brown skin
to her tenant from Hong Kong
as if I were her daughter,
as if she were you.

How do I say I miss you
your scolding
your presence
your roast loin of pork
more succulent, more tender
than any hotel chef's?

The fur coat you wanted
making you look like a polar bear
and the mink-trimmed coat
I once surprised you
on Christmas morning.

Mama, how you said "importment"
for important,
your gold tooth flashing
an insecurity you dared not bare,
wanting recognition
simply as eating noodles
and riding in a motor car
to the supermarket
the movie theater
adorned in your gold and jade
as if all your jewelry
confirmed your identity
a Chinese woman in America.

How you said "you better"
always your last words
glazed through your dark eyes
following me fast as you could
one November evening in New York City
how I thought "Hello, Dolly!"
showed you an America
you never saw.

How your fear of being alone
kept me dutiful   in body
resentful in mind.
How my fear of being single
kept me
from moving out.

How I begged your forgiveness
after that one big fight
how I wasn't wrong
but needed you to love me
as warmly as you hugged strangers.

When I Was Growing Up

AWAY FROM THE BLUE SWANS

Away, away from the blue swans.   Silver, pink?
I remember.   In pairs, swimming across
a wallpaper sea in the upstairs bedroom.

Away and down a mahogany banister
out of Chinatown
where beancakes gleamed in flyspecked windows,
out of opium arms, out of men's hands,
pomade slick, caressing us with nickels and dimes.

Away, away from antlers,
dried lizards' necks,
hidden like pearls in herbalists' shelves,
women warbling Chinese songs, their voices drifting
out the hot summer air,
hanging onto men in grey felt hats
with silver dollars jangling in their pants pockets.

Crossing the boundaries
to the T&D on 11th and Broadway
past Jack's foot-long hot dogs,
smelling popcorn at the antics
of Abbott & Costello.

Arm in arm, our bravery
slung by our mother's warnings
uptown to the Paramount
all its silver and purple
and red velvet carpets
chewing spearmint
through the double feature
and returning to Chinatown
sucking preserved plums
and agreeing to lie

how we laughed at Abbott & Costello,
the Fat Man and Frankenstein
but dreaming the dance
of "Orchestra Wives"

how George Montgomery
on the life-sized screen
sealed our exodus
with his sensuous lips.

REMINISCING ABOUT A CHINESE RESTAURANT

Last night I ate dinner
in a Chinese restaurant,
roast pork and mashed potatoes,
rice and corn, a wedge of custard pie.

Others were eating rice
with beancake and cha siu.
One man ate corned beef and cabbage
and shimmering jello cubes.

Glasses clang, silverware shook,
oil sizzled to another Chinese restaurant,
to Chinatown, a girl

who washed glasses, wiped forks, knives and spoons,
who typed the next day's menu
who squeezed oranges for juice,
large, small,
but always fresh.

In the back kitchen in the damp air
a man bakes apple pies and banana shortcakes.
A cigarette dangles from his mouth,
his eyes half closed.
When his afternoon off comes,
he shuffles off to his rented room,
pulls up his sleeve, sticks
a needle into his arm.

He escapes, orange, delicious,
and I run upstairs, stuff myself
with strawberry pie.
My skin rises in hives,
my skin wants orange, wants delicious.

I awaken.   More dishes, more menus.
I refill the sugar jars.
Granules sparkle, I cover them up
and salt shakers take precedence
on the formica counter
in wooden booths.

Slide and run, run and hide,
wait on those who inhabit
this Chinese restaurant:

A man with a crutch and one leg
limps downstairs from the Aloha Hotel,
sips his dinner of black coffee
and sugared "bombs."

A shriner and his wife, with wide smiles,
eat halibut steak, rice and gravy
and apple pie.
The shriner shakes his tassel with authority.
He splits one 60¢ dinner
for his two young daughters.

Three slices of wholewheat bread
for a glass-eyed customer
who smears catsup on each slice,
thick, juicy, oozing over the plate.
This man paints red in my father's eyes
who shouts to me:
Give him the bottle with the quarter-inch catsup
or we will not survive
we will not survive.

A young gypsy girl and a sallow old man
sit in the back booth.
He lifts her skirt, caresses
her thigh, feeds her a spoon of rice.
She shivers.   I look away.

A gas station attendant peeps
behind the American menu,
one eye on the other waitress.
His lips parted, he orders leg of lamb
with mint jelly.
His money is good, is green.
He pays to eat and look
at the other waitress.

And I eat and my skin itches,
knows nothing, not its hives,
its question marks.

I return to this Chinese restaurant
its blinking coffee-cup neon sign.
I read the menu, examine it
inside out.   The ink spills,
the calligraphy sprawls.

This Chinese restaurant demands love,
demands attention.   Its walls expand,
I slither inside.

What would the glasses, the ovens
and chopsticks tell, what grease
on uniforms, what language
beyond food?

WHERE ARE YOU GOING?

Where are you going now?
Why don't you stay home
and clean the house?

How will you learn
to catch
a husband
if you do nothing on Saturdays
but hang out
at the beauty parlor
then shop all day
to adorn your body?

Why don't you
watch me
cook rice
wash windows
scrub floors
darn sox?

Why don't you?

I am only your mother
I am getting old
Don't you see these white hairs?

Soon I will be in my grave
and even if you get married
and even if you get married
and bear me a grandson
and bear me a grandson
it will have the name, the name, the name
of a stranger,
stranger,
stranger.

WHEN I WAS GROWING UP

I know now that once I longed to be white.
How?   you ask.
Let me tell you the ways.

> when I was growing up, people told me
> I was dark and I believed my own darkness
> in the mirror, in my soul, my own narrow vision.

> > when I was growing up, my sisters
> > with fair skin got praised
> > for their beauty and I fell
> > further, crushed between high walls.

> when I was growing up, I read magazines
> and saw movies, blonde movie stars, white skin,
> sensuous lips and to be elevated, to become
> a woman, a desirable woman, I began to wear
> imaginary pale skin.

> > when I was growing up, I was proud
> > of my English, my grammar, my spelling,
> > fitting into the group of smart children,
> > smart Chinese children, fitting in,
> > belonging, getting in line.

> when I was growing up and went to high school,
> I discovered the rich white girls, a few yellow girls,
> their imported cotton dresses, their cashmere sweaters,
> their curly hair and I thought that I too should have
> what these lucky girls had.

> > when I was growing up, I hungered
> > for American food, American styles
> > coded: *white*   and even to me, a child
> > born of Chinese parents, being Chinese
> > was feeling foreign, was limiting,
> > was unAmerican.

when I was growing up and a white man wanted
to take me out, I thought I was special,
an exotic gardenia, anxious to fit
the stereotype of an oriental chick

>when I was growing up, I felt ashamed
>of some yellow men, their small bones,
>their frail bodies, their spitting
>on the streets, their coughing,
>their lying in sunless rooms
>shooting themselves in the arms.

when I was growing up, people would ask
if I were Filipino, Polynesian, Portuguese.
They named all colors except white, the shell
of my soul but not my rough dark skin.

>when I was growing up, I felt
>dirty.   I thought that god
>made white people clean
>and no matter how much I bathed,
>I could not change, I could not shed
>my skin in the gray water.

when I was growing up, I swore
I would run away to purple mountains,
houses by the sea with nothing over
my head, with space to breathe,
uncongested with yellow people in an area
called Chinatown, in an area I later
learned was a ghetto, one of many hearts
of Asian America.

I know now that once I longed to be white.
How many more ways?   you ask.
Haven't I told you enough?

WITH PARADISE IN MIND

So close to paradise a round-trip ticket
clutched in my hands.   I expected to waltz
down a church aisle in pink taffeta,
plumeria leis around my neck.   To feast
at my friend's wedding, my opportunity
to kiss a dream riding on waves, silver
as the movies had promised.

And how I wept, my father,
that distant August, when I cancelled
my airline reservations
postponing paradise
as you lay dying.

OF NECESSITY

I was a procrastinator of necessity.
I left dust on the venetian blinds, balls of wool
bunched on the fading rug, my baby nephew in his crib
crying, his breakfast on the mattress of blue and white ticking.

At age 5 I hesitated to cross the street
but I ran from Lincoln School, from the kindergarten
where Miss Effie Chew showed us how to cook berry jam
and eat with soda crackers, how to stir and watch
the red bubbling in a crockery pot. Normally I would not
have crossed the street by myself, heeding the warning
of moving cars but the yellow signal flashed me across.

Sleeping late until one.   No, until two o'clock on Saturdays,
on Sundays, telling myself the sun was my enemy, so I obliged
its intimidation and my father's and mother's expectations
that going to college would cost too much.   Besides,
a girl becomes a wife, a mother, and only works
until that magic time.   They convinced me
fate was a precious gift in disguise.

Believing in magic I procrastinated writing poems,
dissecting frogs, dancing on stage, never thought
beyond tradition, the world as my parents, mirroring
the self through others, living vicariously the life
of movie stars, punishing my body
by starving the mind.

I sat at walnut desks, awaiting spells
of sugar and fruit.   And though I saved money to travel,
buy clothes and cover my face, I fell, content
to bask in compliments, drinking scotch and smoking
to prove my adaptability.

Dreams I never found carried me, a dandelion, a guilt,
squealing, hoping someone would hear me.
Guidelines were properties of others, my salvation.
When I prayed in the dark, in my bed, it was for someone to love me,
believing the walls and curtains would never betray
my secret murmurings.

Rain, the sun, the wind, how these elements intruded,
how I murdered myself, believing there was no self,
content to ride the tide of obliteration
not realizing that losses would encroach on my time,
that nourishment must be fed from the self
through dreams, through lethargy,
knowing now one step at a time
is the only possibility.

ON THINKING OF PHOTOGRAPHING MY FANTASIES

No, please don't,
don't photograph me
in my fantasies,
in my orange kimono
with blue and yellow chrysanthemums,
you might see
my legs
with roadmaps
leading
nowhere but down
to the toes
then up to my navel
where little hairs hide
and rise
to my breasts
spaces apart
to my arms
to my eyes
red from smog
my hair black yet greying.
Oh, yes, my fantasies,
lounging in a wicker chair,
posing nude, perhaps,
a cigarette dangling
from my lips
as I sit beneath palm leaves
beaded glass curtains
the wind swishing
mosquitos and gnats
onto my body
itching my fingers
wanting cool wine
wiping ants
off tiled drainboards
out into the garden
where the moon hides
between limbs
of the peony tree
into the courtyard
where mothers of my mother

might have scaled,
shuffling in tiny bound feet
to be sold
to feed
their families,
where the peasants and farmers
raise water buffalo, plant rice,
their backs stooped
to the sun and only after dark
nibble watermelon seeds
and the fathers of my father
separated from the mothers of my mother
gambling, drinking in cities perhaps
after toiling
in sundrenched fields
eating smiles of peach-skinned women
who fan them with feathers
marriages endured
for the paper names of families
across the miles
for crates of canned milk
and apricot nectar
and the music of lutes
of harps and mandolins
scarcely heard
in the ears of peasants
but in dreams and visions
of imperial life
beyond compounds
of water cranked from wells
of cooking rice
to wash the feet
and faces of husbands' parents
who take in daughters-in-law
for muscles
moving daybreak to dusk
where ghosts lurk
in beds of straw mattings
in the orchid bodies of women
who know no poems

but their own lives
for keeping their eyes
leveled at the ground
grateful for not being drowned
or sold
in the shells
of watergourds
allowing the past
the mythologies
to stream forth
like milk from mothers' breasts
into bamboo hollows
time machines flying
like golden phoenixes
telling story after story
to ears untrained for the onslaught
of droughts, monsoons, thunder
where villagers eat pork
if the meat-man comes by,
dirt roads
leading out
to green, the underside
of oceans and skies
where skin and bones
collide with stars
what eyes refuse
to see, what mouths refuse
to talk, tongues cut in infancy
for golden retreats
for the intimacy
of people who think
they know you
because you know
not yet your selves
for lacquer, for brass,
for snow-flower plums
salivating your mouth
and the fuzzy squash
of days and nights
fisted in gnarled hands
and legs just learning

to walk
on levees
on lakes
and rainwashed forests
for the light
of small clearings
where your heart
hones your mind,
the silver bolt
you now hold
in your moving hands

WHERE IS MY COUNTRY?

Where is my country?
Where does it lie?

The 4th of July approaches
and I am asked for firecrackers.
Is it because of my skin color?
Surely not because
of my husband's name.

In these skyways
I dart in and out.
One store sells rich ice cream
and I pick bittersweet nuggets.

In the office someone asks me
to interpret Korean,
my own Cantonese netted
in steel, my own saliva.

Where is my country?
Where does it lie?

Tucked between boundaries
striated between dark dance floors
and whispering lanterns
smoking of indistinguishable features?

Salted in Mexico
where a policeman speaks to me in Spanish?
In the voice of a Chinese grocer
who asks if I am Filipino?

Channeled in the white businessman
who discovers that I do not sound Chinese?
Garbled in a white woman
who tells me I speak perfect English?
Webbed in another
who tells me I speak with an accent?

Where is my country?
Where does it lie?

Now the dress designers flood us
with the Chinese look,
quilting our bodies in satin
stitching our eyes with silk.

Where is my country?
Where does it lie?

LOTUS AS A CHINESE SYMBOL

Not by chance I visited a gift store
just five blocks beyond the stone lion gateway.
In glass cases and wooden shelves, ivory rabbits
and cranes, carved buffalo, bamboo plaques
of flowering plum, even embroidered wedding skirts
of black satin, stained underskirts
worn perhaps in old China.

Is that old, I ask, pointing to a jade lotus
nested in a ball of cotton.
Green, muddy, cloudy,
shaped like a flower I'd never seen
with tiny holes for stringing ornaments,
coral beads, cloisonne.

The saleslady nodded and wrapped the lotus
in a yellow silk purse.   This new treasure
under my arm, I returned to my office,
wondering about its symbol.

At home in a book of Chinese folk designs
the lotus is a flower of summer, of the seventh month,
creative power, purity amid adverse surroundings
and finally, it is a symbol of feminine genius.

Oh, jade lotus (or are you soapstone) around my neck,
what magic, what aura do your petals hold?
What power did this modern woman buy?
Did Mother pick lotus flowers when she was young?
Why did Father love lotus root for cooking soup?
And why did I once buy a lotus pod
for the seeds rattling inside?

I hunger for the symbol, its suggestion, its song,
its life giving essence, contemplative as I am,
peeling, smelling a navel orange.

And yes, I know, I know
there are no Chinatowns in China
and I kowtow, a question mark,
before my parents' graves, here
in the earth that is America.

It's in the Blood

SPECIAL DELIVERY

An old woman
(could be my mother,
could be my sister)
stands at the corner
of Jackson and Grant Avenue
waving her arms at tourists and shoppers
with bags of oranges and bock choy.

The sun shines on her face
and her bright eyes fulfill
the expectations of her audience:
She is crazy,
she is just old,
she does not know
what she is doing,
what she is saying.

(Where are her daughters,
where are her sons?)

Out of a crumpled brown bag
I bite and chew on my hom foon
and try not to stare
behind my dark glasses.

This old woman
(could be my mother,
could be my sister)
talking incoherently
in the sun's eye.

With her plastic shopping bag
and her gold-coin bracelet,
she asks the women
who dig at mounds of grapefruit,
she asks the hatless men
who sneer at her, grinning

What will they do with her
now that Chiang is dead,
now that they crisscross her
to line up in the rush
at Citizens Savings?

BREAKFAST AT THE LEMON TREE

I scoop my poached egg with a piece of rye toast.
A white man sits next to me, orders two eggs, well cooked.
Looking at the menu, he shakes his head, muttering:
I can't get used to American food.

He is well dressed, wears gold bangles, rings.
He speaks carefully as if his lines are rehearsed.

The waitress serves him eggs and hash browns.
The eggs look overcooked, but the man pokes a fat finger
into them and tells the waitress in a loud voice:
I want these eggs dry.

I am almost finished with my breakfast.
The man begins to tell me
how he loves Japanese food.
He tells me he especially loves raw fish.
I get the feeling he is telling me this
because he thinks I am Japanese.

The man talks endlessly.   All this time
his eggs are getting cold.   I wonder
if he intends to eat. Humoring him
I finally ask if he likes cooked fish.
He says he prefers his fish raw.
He stresses "raw" as if toothpicks
pry his mouth open.

I want to tell him about black bass
steamed with green onion and ginger root,
about stuffed fishballs

but he continues talking
about buying a rice cooker
about teaching his landlord how to cook rice
about teaching his landlord
how to eat Japanese food.

IT'S IN THE BLOOD

We never asked to be mysterious.
We never asked to be inscrutable.
Still untold stories, untold histories.
Still the unknown unknown.
Retrieve burnt letters, receipts, bills,
anything written, anything spoken?
Our dreams in bones and ashes?
To be seen and heard.
To be known but not merely by our many names.
Being presumptuous I speak for myself.
Others who remain silent own their own tongues.

Li Hong's ma ma died when Li Hong was an infant.
Ma said that Li Hong's ma ma was a little crazy.
The villagers said so.   Li Hong likes to eat chicken feet.
Li Hong smiles, a childwoman.
Li Hong loves babies.
Li Hong is my sister.

Li Keng remembers Angel Island, the bright lights
of Oakland and San Francisco.
She said that Bah Bah sent fruit and candy
to cheer them up behind bars.
They were lucky, imprisoned
on Angel Island only four days.
The other immigrants waved goodbye,
some etched poems into the walls.
Li Keng learned to eat cheese and tomatoes
on the President Hoover.
To this day Li Keng cannot stomach butter or milk.
Li Keng is my sister.

Lai Wah remembers the ship.   She was three years old.
The immigration officer asked her: What is your name?
Lai Wah answered: If you don't tell me yours,
I won't tell you mine.
Lai Wah smiled behind straight bangs.
Lai Wah remembers nothing of her years in China.
Lai Wah is my sister.

Seow Hong Gee is my father.
Suey Ting Yee Gee is my mother.
From 1933 to 1965 Suey Ting Gee was known as Theo Quee Gee,
a sister's name, a sister's paper that Bah Bah bought
to bring his wife and daughters over.
Theo Quee Gee was supposed to be my father's sister,
my sister's aunt.
This was 1933.   In 1924 the law said that Chinese men
could bring no wives to the United States.
Theo Quee Gee was unmarried but we knew better.

Nellie Wong is my name.   I was never Nellie Gee
but we knew better.
When my sister's aunt, that is, Theo Quee Gee, my mother,
got pregnant, to bear a child out of wedlock
was out of the question.
So Theo Quee Gee got married, by faking
a marriage certificate, by *marrying* a man
named Sheng Wong who agreed to appear
on paper to be my father.
Shame to the outside world avoided.
Secrets depending on which side of the fence.
When I was five and entered Chinese school,
Lai Oy became my Chinese name.

Leslie Wong was born after me.
Ai yah, another girl!   That was my mother's wail.
Ma and Bah Bah named Leslie Li Ying.
Her nick name was *thlom gawk ngon*,
three-corner eye.
Leslie Wong is my sister.

Florence Wong was born after Leslie.
Ai yah, another girl!   That was my mother's wail.
So no more Li's, so no more daughters
with Chinese names beginning with Li,
beginning with *beautiful*.
So Florence was named Ling Oy to change my mother's luck.
Florence Wong is my sister.

William Wong was born after Florence.
Finally a boy!   That was Ma's and Bah Bah's joy.
Thankful their daughter, Ling Oy,
brought them their son.
Bah Bah gave a month-old party
to shave William's head.
Eggs were dyed red, friends and relatives filled the house.
We drank chicken whiskey, gnawed vinegar pigs' feet.
Ling Oy was the magic that Ma and Bah Bah decided.
To beget (a son), to beget (a son) to love
and the heavens answered.
Wah Keung is William Wong's Chinese name.
William Wong is my brother.

I was never sure who I really was.
My school records showed that I was Nellie Wong,
that my father and Leslie's father
and Florence's father and William's father
was a man named Sheng Wong.
We told no lies, only the truth
as we were forced to.

My three older sisters were supposed to be my cousins.
My father was supposed to be my uncle.
My mother was supposed to be my father's sister.
When Theo Quee Gee *confessed* her illegal status,
she became Suey Ting Gee, my father's legal wife.
But it was too late.   Bah Bah died in 1961.

Now I use the name, Nellie Wong.
Now I search for all the names that gave me life.

HOW TO GUARD OUR DEAD?

> "We must guard our dead.   Our enemies
> might disinter them, steal them. . . ."
> Yannis Ritsos, *The Graves of Our Ancestors*

Even now I am hungry
after coffee, toast, eggs and orange juice.
Even now with my belly
invading my tan leather belt.
Even now as I verify figures, change records,
plan multiple itineraries, answer the phones.

The hunger more than for food alone,
more than for odors of ginger, garlic, fish
for I must approach the enemy lines,
link arms with my people
to guard our dead.

Who will steal my mother's bones, my father's ashes?
Who will disinter them one day, ship them to Toishan?
Who will receive them in a festival of bells, cymbals,
the air bursting with firecrackers, my great-grandparents,
their children, aunts and uncles, my unknown cousins?
Who will disinter them and throw them away,
by pieces, fragments, crumbs,
even chains and necklaces?
How to guard our dead to protect ourselves,
how to drink slowly the liquids of our being,
and flow with the rivers of unknown lands,
the mountains and precipices we've never climbed?

Will descendants with breastplates and shields, with swords and masks
chase the enemy, tantalize them
with leaves of lettuce, red envelopes of silver coins?
Will they revive my ancestors' spirits, their valiant struggles,
spread the hilly plains with plump cooked chickens,
see the clipped grass bending,
the wind opening their tombs,
see our people rise
alive as animals thundering in the skies?

SONG FOR MY FATHER: IN FOUR PHOTOGRAPHS

In my arms I carry you upstairs
to the yellow room
and place your photographs
against the wall.

In the first you are a young boy, ten perhaps.
You look away from the camera.
Your Mandarin collar frames your tender face
your hair a cap of peach fuzz.
In this photograph, as in the others, your lips are pressed.
Your right eye is smaller than your left.
In what studio, near or far from your home village,
was this photograph taken?
Did Ngin Ngin bribe you with a jelly sweet?
Did you swat gnats from Ngin Ngin's back?
Did you cool your feet in the village pond?

In the second picture you look austere
your nose fuller, jaw determined.
You are buttoned, still, in a Mandarin jacket,
the buttons mother-of-pearl or wooden, large as quarters.
Your hair is swept to the right, the fuzz
grown out.   You look straight ahead
at the camera, at me.
An official imprint is stamped
beneath the tip of your left ear, a half moon shadowed
on your left jaw.
Your passport, I am sure, my father,
to the United States, a young man, sixteen,
to work in granduncle's herb store
in Oakland's Chinatown.

Now in the third you continue to look ahead.
Your jaw is rounder, softer, and the studio light
focuses your high hairline, shaped a tilted heart.   You wear a tie.
a slash of color, a western shirt, striped, starched.
You sailed three times back to Kwangtung
once to marry my mother, the others to father my sisters.
Then in autumn of 1933 you returned
to Kwangtung for the last time.

You look blank.
If someone should ask me, your fourth daughter,
your first born in the United States,
I would say yes, he looks blank
but I assure you his mind whirls
the rims of four-flavor soup
with tiger lily, lotus seeds, loving hands.

And now, Father, in your fourth photograph
you smile not widely, not a cheshire cat.
You have peddled vegetables from a truck,
run a lottery, welded for Bethlehem Steel,
owned a small grocery, fathered two more daughters,
and finally one son.

Later in our Great China Restaurant you bought
crates of lettuce, baskets of beansprouts.
You beat jello, dittoed menus,
washed floors until midnight.
Your fingers flew on the abacus
as you kept books in your step-down office.

Your hair has thinned, my brows thick as yours,
brushstrokes I've tried to control.
You wear a grey suit, vested,
a white shirt.
Your eyes, two lights
shining on my typing fingers.

How can I explain the kind of man you were,
the kind of father
who delivered our raincoats and galoshes
to the office at Lincoln School
when only a hint of rain would fall?

How can I explain how you lost your car
returning drunk from a tong banquet
sure you had left it locked
on a familiar street?

How can I explain how you shouted
at our customers, embarrassing me,
intensity, endurance, badges
of one Chinaman's life?

How can I explain how you spanked
your grandchildren with your own loving cry,
"haw........pock!" chasing them
until they laughed?

You stare at me, my father, and I stare back.
What would you think, what would you say
now if you knew I wrote you and dreamed you,
wanting touch, gold, your aroma?

This, this yellow room washes me ashore
from a distant sea where you grew up
you who gathered us together on your Wednesday night off
feeding us squab in lettuce cups
telling us, somehow
that love is brewed in iron pots
if we but reach in beyond lobster shells
the bones of chicken feet
if we but stand among reeds
and fly
even with our hands in dishwater,
our legs mirrored in a city lake
watching ducks and pigeons eat
and laughing together at your knees.

In your boxer shorts you waltz
through the living room
fragrant, thick as wood fungus.

THE DEATH OF LONG STEAM LADY

If Paisley Chan had her way, she would not go to Long Steam Lady's funeral.   But of course she must.   If she didn't go, she couldn't forgive herself.   Besides, she loved Long Steam Lady and she missed seeing the old woman sitting in the sun in Portsmouth Square.   Long Steam Lady with her plastic shopping bag filled with bock choy, carrots and sometimes a roll or two of pressed crab apples.   Long Steam Lady with her painted eyebrows and fat red lips which even made them thicker, more sensuous than Paisley thought she should have colored them.   But who was she, Paisley Chan, to say, to judge how Long Steam Lady dressed, how Long Steam Lady decorated herself?   Even in an old flowered nylon dress and a tattered wool coat, Long Steam Lady looked elegant, with her eyes closed, letting the sun beat down on her unlined face, her unwrinkled hands.

Paisley dressed herself slowly and deliberately.   What to wear to a Chinese funeral these days?   Though Paisley was not a blood relative, she would wear sensible navy blue, or perhaps her coffee-brown pantsuit and her beige polyester blouse, the one she could tie into a puffy bow.   Yes, she'd look tailored, dignified, and she would not wear lipstick.   Yes, she'd walk into Gum Moon Funeral Parlor at the edge of Portsmouth Square, and no one would know her.   Paisley Chan, thirty six years old.   Paisley Chan, who worked as a telephone receptionist in the Financial District for nineteen years.   Paisley Chan, who discovered Long Steam Lady looking grand in a frayed purple cloche in Portsmouth Square, who found herself having lunch with a talkative old woman for the past three months, who found it refreshing to leave her office every day at lunch, a reprieve from the enforced sterility of saying, "Good morning, J & C Enterprises," as if she were a machine.

Paisley ran a tortoise comb through her thick curly hair.   Then she grabbed an Afro comb and separated several stubborn strands, letting them curl away from her scalp, then watched the hair form commas, curving into each other like a chorus line of dancers in a dream.   Long Steam Lady had told Paisley that she had been a dancer, a dancer at Imperial City, which was now a disco.   Whether that was true Paisley didn't know and she didn't care.   She loved sitting in Portsmouth Square listening to Long Steam Lady spin her stories of how she slithered in sequined gowns, how she danced in top hats and tails, how she tap danced, how she tangoed with her lover-partner, Alexander Hing, and how she never rose from bed until one o'clock in the afternoon after an exhausting performance.

One day when Paisley was nibbling on hom foon and getting her fingers all sticky, she asked Long Steam Lady how she got her name. Long Steam, *cheong hay*, a talker, a blabbermouth. "Why are you called *Cheong Hay Poa*?" Paisley had asked, licking her fingers and relishing the grease from the filled rice noodles. Several pigeons clustered at Paisley's and Long Steam Lady's feet, pecking at seeds that Long Steam Lady spread lovingly on the ground as she pantomimed a folk dance of planting rice for the autumn harvest.

Paisley had watched the old woman with wonder, with awe. "Well, aren't you ever going to tell me your real name?" Paisley had asked impatiently. "I really want to know. Is it Estelle, Miranda, Sylvia?" The old woman closed her eyes for a moment, ignoring the beautiful names that her young companion had tossed at her like newly burst fireworks. "Ah, *Nu*, that doesn't matter. No names matter, don't you know that? I am Long Steam Lady. I am *Cheong Hay Poa* because I talk too much. I talk so much that no one ever listens to me, and no one listens to me because they can't make sense of what I say. Who has time?" She shrugged her shoulders. "I talk about everything, this and that about love, not just worrying where my body will be laid to rest, whether it will be pointed in the right direction of heaven's blessing. Ah, no, life is too short to worry about dying when all one has to do is to love. No name, child, just Long Steam Lady, just *Cheong Hay Poa*. That is enough."

Long Steam Lady had refused to continue the discussion any longer. She had begun to spread more seeds on the ground, and more pigeons clustered around her feet, pecking around her worn shoes, not Dr. Scholl's that were high laced, not in somber black leather, but silver sandals that she had danced in when she was young. The heels were badly worn and in need of repair, but somehow Long Steam Lady's legs were still slender, a dancer's legs with strength and vitality. Long Steam Lady had told Paisley she never married. She had only loved Alexander Hing. Yes, Alexander Hing who danced circles around Fred Astaire. Yes, Alexander Hing. Long Steam Lady's eyes got misty, but Alexander Hing already had a wife.

Paisley slipped on her pantyhose and cursed as she had slipped them on backwards. She removed them and began again. She stared out her apartment window and watched the leaves of a pink camellia bush glisten in the sunlight. She watched the nylon panels move lightly in the breeze. Autumn was her favorite season, Halloween, Thanksgiving, homemade oxtail stew and chrysanthemums. Yes, she'd visit Long Steam Lady with her spider chrysanthemums though she wasn't sure whether Long Steam Lady would be cremated or buried at Ning Yeong Cemetery at Colma.

Paisley didn't know whether Long Steam Lady had any relatives. Long Steam Lady had mentioned once a sister who lived in New York City. Perhaps Paisley would meet that sister today at the funeral, but Paisley didn't even know her last name. Whom would she ask for? Would she yell out, "Yoo hoo, is Long Steam Lady's sister here from New York City? Long Steam Lady, *Cheong Hay Poa*, the dancer, the old woman who died all alone?" Why that would be downright embarrassing for someone whose name she didn't even know. And if she did find the sister, then what? How would she describe her friendship with the old woman? Lunch friends, companions? Philosophers, sisters? Grandmother, granddaughter?

Paisley sighed, again wishing she didn't have to go to the funeral. She didn't want to see Long Steam Lady lying in her coffin, lifeless, painted grotesquely by morticians who knew nothing about her, morticians who would over-rouge her cheeks, morticians who would redesign her with no creativity, no imagination. If Paisley had her way, she would dress Long Steam Lady in a black gown of airy silk crepe, satin spaghetti straps, with a huge sunburst of rhinestones pinned on one shoulder, with a red silk rose tucked into her bunned hair. But no, the morticians would probably dress her in a wool suit of salt-and-pepper tweed, or in a housedress with droopy lavender flowers, or worse yet, in an old coat sweater with large pockets and military buttons. The mourners would never know Long Steam Lady, the dancer. The mourners would never know, would never see the silver sandals that Long Steam Lady wore daily to the park. They would shake their heads. Women would weep and sniff into their handkerchiefs, and Paisley would hear them say, "Long Steam Lady was a good woman, she never harmed anyone." And she would hear them say, "Ai yah, too bad she never married, never had any sons to look after her in her old age."

Paisley had never heard Long Steam Lady complain about not getting married, about not having sons. Sometimes Long Steam Lady wandered in her conversations. Sometimes she jumped from talking about dancing at Imperial City to looking for a letter written to her from her village in Toishan. But always, Paisley remembered, Long Steam Lady's eyes sparkled, her eyes grew large and luminous as she fell into lapses of memory, smiling as if she harbored the most delicious secret in the world.

And then Long Steam Lady was no more. For the past week Paisley had gone looking for her at the bench nearest the elevator in Portsmouth Square. Paisley took roast beef sandwiches and Bireley's orange drinks as if those items would seduce Long Steam Lady's appearance from the dark. Even the pigeons clustered closer to Paisley as she searched for the slender old woman among the crowds of men huddled in their games, among children laughing and running from their mothers, among the men who exercised Tai Chi Chuan, among the shoppers who spilled out into the park.

Paisley kicked herself for not knowing where Long Steam Lady lived. It had to be somewhere in Chinatown, perhaps at Ping Yuen, perhaps up Jackson or Washington Street, or Mason near the cable car barn. But Long Steam Lady, as talkative as she was, never revealed where she slept, never revealed whether she had any relatives looking in on her. But that was what attracted Paisley in the first place. Long Steam Lady's elegance, her dignity, her independence. Though Long Steam Lady must have been at least seventy five, she never walked dragging her feet. She never hunched. She had moved with the agility of a younger person, younger perhaps than Paisley herself. Funny how Long Steam Lady used to call her "Pessalee" instead of Paisley, speaking to her in a mixture of English and Sze Yip dialect, in a language familiar and warm and endurably American. "Hah, hah," Long Steam Lady had laughed, "you have to learn how to jom the cow meat the right way. See, like this, not like that," and she had begun to move her hands in quick vertical rhythms, showing Paisley how to jom cow meat. "See, it's all in the way how you jom. Jomming, it's the best secret."

Of course, Long Steam Lady had to have a name. How else could relatives have arranged the funeral at Gum Moon? How else could mourners order wreaths of carnations and marigolds streaming with white ribbons, with Long Steam Lady's name brushed in black ink? Although Mr. Eng, the florist, had told Paisley that Long Steam Lady's funeral was Saturday, he never said Long Steam Lady's name. He had said he read her obituary in the *Gold Mountain Times*. Paisley rose from her vanity and searched through a stack of *Chronicles* on her hall table. It had never occurred to her to look through the obituaries in the *Chronicle*, but if there were services for Long Steam Lady, it had to be in the *Chronicle* too. Paisley flipped through the last three days' papers.

Nothing on Long Steam Lady, nothing on names such as Wong, SooHoo, Young, Lee, Fong, Chin. Nothing on former dancers at Imperial City, on old women who fed pigeons in Portsmouth Square. On old men who died alone in their rooms. Not that Chinese people didn't die, not that waiters, laundrymen, seamstresses, dishwashers didn't die. Paisley lingered over an article on the death of a philanthropist, a member of the Pacific Union Club, a world-wide traveler, a grandfather of twelve, a civil servant. And if an obituary had appeared in the *Chronicle* on Long Steam Lady, would they have identified her as a talkative crazy old lady who fed pigeons in the park? Would they have described her silver sandals?

Well, she'd go to the funeral, she owed Long Steam Lady that. It didn't matter to Paisley that she wouldn't know any of Long Steam Lady's relatives. Who knows? Perhaps Alexander Hing might be there, an old Alexander Hing in his tapdancing shoes, an old Alexander Hing whose hair might still be black and shiny as Long Steam Lady had described him, whose pencil-thin mustache tickled Long Steam Lady as they kissed? Paisley smiled and pushed her bangs out of her eyes. Long Steam Lady and she sitting together in Portsmouth Square, laughing and talking loudly. Long Steam Lady and she devouring custard tarts as if they were gold. Long Steam Lady and she scolding panhandlers away from their pink boxes of cha siu bow and hah gow and hom foon.

In the sunlight Paisley walked up Washington Street to Gum Moon Funeral Parlor. She cast her eyes across Portsmouth Square, at the bench where she and Long Steam Lady spent many lunch hours together. She saw pigeons pecking near the garbage can. She saw felt hats, grey suits, plaid shirts. She saw beer cans roll across the pathway. Paisley shifted her gaze and began to daydream about silver sandals. At thirty six perhaps it was not too late to sign up for dancing lessons.

Red Journeys

ENTER THE MIRROR

I have no children. The other night I dreamt I gave birth to an insect. What terrified me even more was that the insect was sucking up a glob of pink goo. Was it a strawberry milkshake? And did it ooze from my vagina? This is not a metamorphosis. This is a dream, and I am perplexed now at age 44 why the process of birthing seeps up through the subconscious at night when the moon should be napping.

In another dream, on another night, a woman rose before me. She was dressed in a cheong sam of white brocade. White orchids spilled from the seams of her dress, cascaded over her mandarin collar, framing her face in an avalanche of snow. However, she was still my friend even with her false eyelashes, thick as woolyworms on the edge of sleep. The only thing that didn't change—from real life, that is—was her long, long hair, black and silver as rain in a late-night movie.

I have no children. I am rushing to complete tasks, chores, adventures, before I die. I am not afraid of death, of dying. I do not separate the joy of typing from the necessity of walking, the euphoria of plotting from the attraction of fighting. I want to write stories, poems, plays, to write and write and stand by them, tall, no twins or copies, but firsts, until my last breath.

In my bathroom I make up songs. I watch my movements in the three-way mirror, my feet cool as icicles on the cobalt-blue tile. I enter the mirror and other selves emerge from arms that fling, a cabaret chanteuse, from a mouth that blossoms, not in a trance, but in rhythm with my pounding heart.

When I was young, I wanted to dance. I wanted to foxtrot with Fred Astaire, tapdance with Gene Kelly, tango with Tony Wing, swing with Cyd Charisse, and even then I was dancing, dancing toward death. Is death an obsession, an occupation? Or is it life, is it every waking moment when the spark titillates the brain and the premises, conflicts, and characters blink themselves from eye-flashes, from dreams and desire to be a chameleon, yet human, and yet be free? Once I said to my youngest sister that we were dying the moment we were born. "How morbid," she responded, and I laughed.

I have no children. I am a tutor. Linda is 13 and reads at third grade level, fifth month. Linda won't show me the dances she knows, but she likes to dance as much as she likes to rollerskate. Linda lost her personal dictionary which she was filling with new words: *energy, hippopotamus, illusion, rainfall, desolation, adventure.*   She also lost her No. 2 pencils inscribed with "Eagle Mirado" which I stole from work. Linda will read.   She will like to read by the end of spring.   I will see to it.   I will plot a story of brother "Q" and sister "U," convince her of their golden links, of the magic of images more magnificent than all of the gumballs enclosed in an antique machine.

I have no children, but the doorsteps, the light streaming through the transom . . . will tomorrow be concrete if I work and wait to jog around Lake Merritt and let the wind carry me, extinct and fleet as a pterodactyl?   And just now my boss puts up a poster on my file cabinet. In the poster an alligator is sneaking up.   An alligator is actually tip-toeing in the grass, behind a great white hunter who is lost in his binoculars.   The words on the poster leap at me in firecracker red: "Mistakes usually happen when we're not paying attention.   Let's concentrate."

And when Dick from Portland Sales calls inquiring about Arnold Mfg., he says, "Arnold Mfg. in San Francisco."   But my boss insists that Dick was inquiring about Mr. Arnold of Morgan Mfg.   I don't tell my boss that I suspect my brains are scissors.

And two weeks ago when I took a message from a customer in Honolulu, I told my boss to call Mr. Arthur Oka.   Who?   Mr. Arthur Oka.   That's what the voice from the island said.   Waves crashed in my ears.   My secretarial voice was firm.   I can be a mule, or I can be a tiger.   Now when Mr. Asaoka calls, I am friendly, I address him by his first name.   I chat about the unusual February heat, the coming summer fog, but I don't tell him that I am a poet.   I don't even tell him about my dreams.

TOWARD A 44TH BIRTHDAY

Mornings and eggshells crack, the eggshells scatter
to the wind.   You carry them within you, the wind,
and lift your feet toward construction sites and know
that construction men eye women from the corners
of their eyes.   Silence sniffs at you like a cat
and still you walk toward work, toward skyscrapers,
imagine the shattering of old plateglass.   You forget
the Ko-Rec-Type, the carbon copies, the Xerox machines.
The timeclock ticks, a medallion on the wall.   You dream
of grinding coffee beans, relaxing in the hot sun of Egypt,
forget that the pyramids are a wonder of the world.
Is it another vacation you need, apple trees to sit
under, the longings of a girl searching for arms,
hands to link to her tiny fingers?   You sigh, reading
of diamonds in millionaires' teeth, of maids tidying
beds for other maids, of a Luckys strikebreaker being struck
by a car.   No, not a car, but a driver, a human being.
What life will you find in your roamings toward China,
toward Asian America in its kitchens crowded with dreams,
on its streets teeming with cracks, toward young men
being tried for killings at the Golden Dragon, toward
pioneer women of the 19th century, the pioneer women
who live within your bones and the voice of Siu Sin Far
nudges you awake.   How far, how near will sisters talk?
Will art atrophy, will it become the tools in our hands?

A WOMAN AT THE WINDOW

sees herself in a white silk linen blazer,
a black skirt with a slit, a cinnabar-red blouse,
and she sees herself through the plateglass
standing there with her hands thrust deep
into her pockets standing there watching the sun
sparkle in a thousand lights in pools of silver needles
as she wanders in search of memories
As usual the sun intrudes her darkness
her feelings of aloneness and privacy
and when the phone rings she dashes
to answer it, changes her mood from aloneness
to sounding office official sounding
like the secretary she is
though sometimes she forgets that she is a poet
and prefers to stand at the window, imagine
herself a mannequin in a shop window
posing with a vacuous stare with her hands extended
like hammers ready to crash through the plateglass
breaking loose from the wool and the silk
from the neon lights the store decorator
has knotted around her neck
If she crashes through the window she would
see blood dripping from her fingers
but she wouldn't lick them
she doesn't always like to taste red
but she knows the violence that is contained
inside her body as she feels trapped
like a silver fox desired for her skin
to be worn by a woman who passes her by
She knows instinctively that she is a woman
who wants to float in and out of other skins
a witch, a princess, a bag lady, a diem sum shop girl,
her mother dying of cancer, her grandmother who feeds
pigeons in the park, or a sewing factory woman
who plans to organize for higher wages,
for music and bright lights, for time to play
with her infant daughter

She doesn't understand her feelings of floating
water hyacinths or lilies
as a dragon imbued with powers
as wind that rages through her limbs
as a lion at the electric typewriter
as a voice of women and men of Asian America
She knows that she isn't alone or lonely
that the memories will find her standing
twenty-three floors above a city lake
that sunlight is her companion that the air
she breathes though filled with pollutants that she will
fight them with the swallowing of antihistamines
that she will fight them, a woman at the window
with her fingers that desire to become wings

RED JOURNEYS

I dream red dreams, an oasis of fire and light.
Big Grandmother calls my mother on the phone
and I answer.   "Ma," I call, "ah Ai Poo wah, she wants
to talk to you," and I filter away, my legs wobble
at the onslaught of tiny white matchbox cars.
Zoom   zoom   zoom   zoom!
Is it a river carrying me away?
Is it the moon who says "no"?   Is it my resistance,
my giving in to a body writhing in the deep, dark night?
Ai Poo and Ma are talking now to each other.
They sing and gossip and share pig's tail soup, but wait!
Big Grandmother has given up meat.   Ma never has.
Ma loved to cook and gather us together
continuing what Bah Bah did, continuing
the tradition of feasting on poor man's food, ricecrusts crackling
in hot boiled water.
My nose tickles.   The white metal cars.
Zoom   zoom   zoom   zoom!
They attack my fingers, my dancing feet.
Do they dare to act powerful as firecrackers?
Do they dare to think, live their own lives?
Are they ghosts wandering in search of bodies,
seeking longevity noodles?   Birthdays, whole chickens poached
for the birth of sons, red egg and ginger parties,
ceremonies for shaving a baby's head.   Birthdays.
And for girls?   And for me?
Oh, Ma.   Oh, Ai Poo.
Are you listening to this daughter's tongue?
Are you singing as you have sung earthmiles away?
And what is filial piety to mothers and grandmothers,
the greatgrandmothers I've never known?
Unbandage these eyes, unbind these feet.   Tell me
what threads memory   dream   myth   reality?

Red quince blooms, oranges and salted fish.
Good luck words ring in my ears.
My walls are indy orange, red flowers sprout in paper cut-outs,
a fireplace I dare not burn.   Framed in mother-of-pearl
a kingfisher dives for pollens from spring buds
embroidered in strands of silk.   And, Ma, your passport
photographs you young and expectant as you must be now.
It's true that girls stay with their mothers forever.
It's true you wept when you left your own mother
and then she fell in Ai Leong while you sailed
across oceans to your new life in America.
Would Poo Poo have loved me and my sisters?
Would she have spoiled us, spanked us?
I put my hands in hers, stroll along paths of flowering peach,
stop with her at a pond and watch the goldfish play
and yet we rise and walk again, step by step, through
atriums and rice fields under the burning sun.   We stop again,
refresh our tongues with tangerines and she would begin
to tell me about you as a girl, how you worked as a bride
to please your mother-in-law.   Your hands, these twin knuckles
crack from the coming Spring.

FOR MY SISTER WHOSE NAME, AMONG OTHERS, IS COURAGE

Who is she?   She lies on the hospital bed.
She vomits, weary from chemotherapy,
fragile as spring narcissus.

She is my sister.   I look at her deeply, quietly.

She serves an ace on the tennis court,
runs her opponent ragged.
She organizes a festival, year after year,
to celebrate Asian Pacific American heritage.

She rises, goes to work.
She serves pancakes and coffee
to customers at the Great China.
She types for Milen's jewelers,
waits on tables at Pland's Restaurant,
serves trays of cocktails at Tiki Bob's.

Meanwhile, after she cooks dinner
for her husband and children,
at midnight she cooks and serves chow mein
to her mother-in-law's friends
who play round after round of mah jongg.

Who is she?   This woman who fights back
with every breath, this woman who is my sister
and I love her.

Her hair grows back.
Fragility is not her nature,
not this sister who raised three children,
this sister who stretches and runs,
who skis, bowls, supervises an office
for the Oakland Unified School District.

She, whose hand links mine,
as we run on the grass at Lake Merritt,
drink our parents' homemade lemonade
served from an aluminum stew pot,
as we hunt for our lost baby brother
as we picnic beneath the redbud, laughing,
holding back our thick long hair.

She is Leslie   ai ng nui   fifth daughter
Thlom Gawk Ngon   three-corner eye
Ah Lessalee   Dragon Teen   Cotton Ball Queen
She is Lai Ying   Beautiful Eagle
breathing   strong   living

MY CHINESE LOVE

My Chinese love does not climb the moongate toward heaven
nor flowers in a garden of peonies and chrysanthemums.
My Chinese love lives in the stare of a man in a coolie hat,
smiling to himself, content in the meanderings of his mind.

My Chinese love lives in the voices of my grandmothers
who don't see me, their granddaughter writing and singing
their joys and sorrows.   Yet they pass me by on the streets,
chattering among themselves, keeping warm in crocheted hats,
carrying plastic yellow sacks of Chinese greens.

Though concubines and priestesses flourished during the dynasties,
they are not my only Chinese love.   My Chinese love cannot be
suppressed in the inequities of the past, cannot be uplifted
only through the love poems of ancient women.   My Chinese love
flourishes in the wails of women selling dried noodles,
in the small hands of their daughters who have been sold.

How American is my Chinese love?   How anxious, how true?
Taxicabs and rickshas whiz through the streets of Hong Kong
as sampans drift along the Mekong while women wash
their families' clothes, greeting me as an American tourist.

My Chinese love wanders in search of dreams and memories,
of visions still unseen.   My Chinese love is noisy, clacks
of mah-jongg tiles rising from basement rooms, permeates
like peanut oil from my mother's kitchen, shines in the bright eyes
of my father who growls and scares
the customers in our Great China Restaurant.

My Chinese love is my uncle whose skin yellowed from a lifetime
of opium addiction, yet who was born whole and pure.
My Chinese love is my curiosity of his young life, how he arrived
a bachelor on America's shores to bake Chinese apple pies.

My Chinese love burns.   It laughs in the voices of children
sharing oranges with their neighborhood friends.
My Chinese love is a warrior.   Physical death cannot swallow
it, banish it from a woman who won't rest
until she exhales the spirit
of each woman, man and child still fighting
to eat and live on this our inherited earth.

UNDER OUR OWN WINGS

For a sister, Merle Woo

Do not despair, my sister, of a brother's process.
Laughter connects to self-examination.
Laughter can be an opium poppy spreading
its poison first among ourselves.   Our selves
our whole selves, fragments, chopped liver
in a gold fish bowl.
To remain private with change is to self-destruct.
To go public with change is to begin
to challenge the forces of white supremacy.
Yet good fortune the good fortune of battles is not
simply opening red envelopes containing coins or paper money.
To believe that change comes about is to keep working.
As someone said, dear sister, as someone said
you are always working, working
hammering away
at lies, myths, distortions
water hyacinths clogging
the canals of Asian America.
Yet we are not property
to be sold, disposed, auctioned off.
What is antique, what is held valuable
is not necessarily unbreakable.   A sea of faces stare
at our invisibility, our supposed assimilation.   A man believes
simply that to err is to be human
and we sit and stir among whites, yellows,
a few friends.
Ears and tongues perceive
the images of history swallowed in antiseptic schoolrooms
on the battles of Vietnam
in the bedrooms, porno movie theaters, magazines, TV screens
of America.
Any wonder, dear sister, any wonder
that sisters and brothers must exorcise through ritual, form,
poems, songs, stories, essays, plays,
at its own pace
the malaise of white America.

To create our own histories, culture,
restore our own bodies to red health
to battle with every warrior beneath our pores.
Though we try   because we must
Though we try   because we want
To control our own destinies we are mirrored
in the windows of clouds
in the shattered glass
of our race and our sex.
How can we separate our race from our sex, our sex from our race?
And we hear again and again we must struggle against racism
at the exclusion of sexism.
And we hear again and again we must struggle against sexism
at the exclusion of racism.
These tactics.   These words I must use, this language, this tiresome
but necessary chant.   We in the midst of struggle would love
to ski downhill and breathe nothing but fresh air.   And I must ask:
how can we stand in isolation, how can we blow away the blasts
of destruction bombarding us from every direction
because we are
women, because we are
colored, because we are
feared?

The sagas of long steam ladies.
The sagas of long steam men,
the talkers, the orators, the dancers
they are here before us, we are here among them
brimming with language, music, air.
We birth ourselves, our privacies exposed,
proud, seemingly free and yet devils poke
at our very bones
to steal the art that is our lives
the magic that is our source
the spring that is our imagination.
To truly create is to struggle.
To truly struggle is to present
our selves, our processes of living, learning
and unlearning the garbage of self-contempt, of self-defeat

heaped at our own doorsteps.   Sometimes we rein in
the blinders, sometimes we see no farther
than our own skins, sometimes we prick
ourselves, savor the cactus of our own pains.
No despair, no struggle, no joy is personal.
If you begin, I begin.
If you breathe, I breathe.
If you sing, I sing.
And our tales are endless, our tales begin
as the heads of dragons soaring
from the depths of our bodies.
To imagine and not only dwell within that imagination.
To live in our own skin and not only peel our own layers.
To join hands does not mean we always touch.
In art we open ourselves.
In art we begin to return to ourselves.
In art we give ourselves our human joys, our struggles.
Nothing falls into our laps, not flower petals in the Spring
not even these letters that type words, language, experience, validation.
The silences break.   The silences swell.   The silences weep
and the skies once mute about our lives
thunder at our insolence, our daring, our strong yellow legs.
Let us thunder and become the wind.
Let our voices howl and let our voices sing.
Let Gold Mountain move and never stop.
In death our bodies regress to the innocence of bones.
In love we work to live in America under our own wings.